The Leadership Lessons of Gregg Popovich

A Case Study of the San Antonio Spurs'

5-time NBA Championship Winning Head Coach

Leadership Case Studies

Leadership Case Studies.

Table of Contents

Introduction

The San Antonio Spurs have been competitive in the NBA for over a decade. Lead by head coach Gregg Popovich, the Spurs won their first NBA championship in 1999. They won their fifth championship 15 years later, all with the same head coach and the same star player in Tim Duncan.

In an industry that has changed drastically over those years, how did Gregg Popovich manage a team that remained competitive for so long? What were the strategies that he employed to win 5 championships and to make the playoffs for 18 straight years? How did he build a culture where everyone is focused on the goals of the team on not on individual recognition?

In this leadership case study, we analyze the team building strategies of Gregg Popovich and the San Antonio Spurs. We discuss the ways that Popovich builds relationships with his players, and how they are able to constantly achieve success.

The lessons from this leadership study on Gregg Popovich and the San Antonio Spurs can be applied to any business, team, or organization. Whether you are a basketball fan or not, the ideas and strategies of this modern-day Renaissance man can help improve the team culture and performance of any organization in a competitive industry.

In Part One of the case study, we focus on the CULTURE of the organization. We discuss how the Spurs are built like a efficient business where each part of the organization is marching towards to same goals. We highlight the unique way Popovich is able to build trust and relationships with his players, and how they are able to identify talent wherever it may be.

Part Two highlights the PERFORMANCE aspect of the San Antonio Spurs. We discuss the work ethic and preparation factors that makes the Spurs being the most fundamentally sound teams in all of professional sports. We also highlight the manner in which Popovich is able to use innovative strategies to exploit changes in the NBA. The case study closes by discussing how the Spurs were able to bounce back from a heartbreaking loss in the 2013 NBA Finals to win the championship the following year.

To help apply the lessons to your own organization, we have included a few review questions after each section.

All information in this case study has been collected from public sources. Links to the articles and source information are available at our website, leadershipcasestudies.com.

Background Information on Gregg Popovich

Date of Birth: January 28, 1949

College Education: Air Force Academy with a degree in Soviet Studies, 1970.

Head Coaching Experience:
Pomona College - Pitzer College (1979-1985, 1986-1987)
San Antonio Spurs (1996-Present)

National Championships and Awards:

San Antonio Spurs (1999, 2003, 2005, 2007, 2014)

NBA Coach of the Year (2003, 2012, 2014)

Part 1: Culture

Organizational Structure

With over a decade of consistent success, the San Antonio Spurs have been praised for their efficiency in running their organization. There are several factors that have contributed to the winning program that has been developed in San Antonio.

In an article posted on International Business Times, Bobby Ilich quotes a business professor explain how the Spurs organization is managed like a high-performing company.

In business, there is a performance model that is based upon "strategy, structure, people, and process," says Terance Wolfe, a clinical management and organization professor at the University of Southern California's Marshall School of Business.

"Strategy is having a clear and compelling goal. The structure is: are we organized to meet that goal? And then, do we have the right people and capabilities? And that doesn't necessarily mean superstars," Wolfe explains. "The process is kind of the glue. It's the culture you create within your organization. It's the reward system. It's the leadership style and coaching style."

In previous years, many sports media analysts and general sports fan stated that the Spurs were boring. Due to the lack of a flashy superstar who would command the highlight reel, the Spurs were a well-respected team but didn't get the television ratings when compared to the Los Angeles Lakers with Kobe Bryant or the Miami Heat and Cleveland Cavaliers with Lebron James.

Ilich compared the Spurs to car maker Toyota, which "was known for saturating suburban communities with unsexy models that regularly won awards for reliability. Only the purist regards the

Spurs as must-see TV, yet with little drama or mystery they keep winning."

One of the key methods that the San Antonio Spurs use to achieve constant success by having stability in its leadership group. Team owner Peter Holt bought into the team in 1996. Gregg Popovich was hired as the head coach during the 1996 season, and RC Buford was named General Manager in 2002.

"The triumvirate of Holt, Popovich, and Buford has produced such positive results that there has been little impetus to rock the boat. This is in sharp contrast to most NBA teams, which often go through multiple coaches and GM in a span of five years let alone a dozen or more," writes Ilich.

To put the stability and long-lasting success of the Spurs into context, Gregg Popovich completed his 19th season as the head coach of the Spurs at the end of the 2015 season. From the 1996-1997 season (when Popovich took over the Spurs) until the 2014-2015 season, here are the number of head coaches for some other teams during that time period.

Los Angeles Lakers: 10
Denver Nuggets: 11
Sacramento Kings: 11
Dallas Mavericks: 4
Houston Rockets: 4

As the Washington Post reported, every other NBA team made at least 2 coaching changes during the time that Popovich has been with the Spurs.

In addition to the leadership group, the core group of players who are the leaders of the team has also been with the Spurs for a long period of time.

Tim Duncan: Drafted in 1997 and has played 18 straight seasons with the team.

Tony Parker: Drafted in 2001 and has played 14 straight seasons with the team.
Manu Ginobili: Joined in 2002 and has played 13 straight seasons with the team.

By having a core group of players led by stable management group has allowed the Spurs to focus on what they need to do each year. There is no concerns about the overall strategy, and the team doesn't change directions each year. Unlike other teams with weak management, there is no internal chaos. Everyone in the organization understands their role, and understands how things are to be done.

But stability does not mean stagnation. Just because the Spurs have the same people leading the team each year does not mean that things don't change. In fact, the Spurs are always adapting to the new environment and finding new ways to win.

Identifying Overlooked Talent

Gregg Popovich and the San Antonio Spurs are not afraid to change things up. Whether it be their tactics on the court to the diversity of their personnel, the organization has the faith in their own culture and management to be able to get people to succeed.

Like any multinational CEO, Gregg Popovich must manage a global workforce. With the popularity of basketball spanning the globe, more and more players in the last three decades have been entering the NBA. Like any industry, the NBA has globalized its workforce and its product.

According to a report in the New York Times, there were 5 players from Eastern Europe in the NBA in 1989, right around the time the Berlin Wall fell. In 1992, when Michael Jordan, Magic Johnson and Larry Bird represented the United States in the Summer Olympics, the NBA had fewer than two dozen international players from 18 countries.

Since then, the NBA has expanded its global reach significantly. As the New York Times reports, the NBA "has opened offices in 14 global markets, played about 145 exhibition and regular-season games in international cities and expanded television coverage to 215 countries and territories, in 47 languages."

In the 2013 season, there were 85 international players on the rosters of NBA teams, representing 36 nations. The first round of the 2013 NBA draft featured 12 international players. In both the 2014 and 2015 drafts, 3 out of the top 5 picks were born outside of the United States.

International players are now common in the league, and the San Antonio Spurs has led the way in finding players who can contribute to a championship caliber team.

Here are the birthplace of members of the championship winning 2013-2014 San Antonio Spurs.

Manu Ginobili, Argentina.
Patty Mills, Australia.
Tiago Splitter, Brazil.
Corey joseph, Canada.
Boris Diaw, France.
Tony Parker, France.
Marco Belinelli, Italy.
Aron Baynes, New Zealand.
Kawhi Leonard, United States.
Danny Green, United States.
Matt Bonner, United States.
Tim Duncan, United States Virgin Islands.

According to Kirk Goldsberry of Grantland, Popovich utilized this diverse group of players so effectively that the 2014 Spurs "were the first team since the ABA-NBA merger in 1976 not to have a single player average more than 30 minutes per game. In other words, Popovich relies on his starters less and his bench more than anybody in decades."

This strategy of utilizing international players is in part based upon necessity. Since the Spurs drafted Tim Duncan with the Number 1 pick in 1997, they have drafted no higher than the 20th pick in the NBA draft. Most of the top United States players have already been selected by the time the Spurs select their pick. However, this works to the favor of the Spurs as the training background of these players are much more in tune with the style of play that the Spurs emphasize.

Jere Longman writes in the New York Times that foreign basketball players "tend to develop in club systems rather than in school-based systems. Thus, there are few limits on practice time compared with American high schools and colleges - or in some cases none."

While in these club systems, the coaching and teaching of the players are much more centralized than the coaching in the United States. There is a much stronger emphasis on everyone learning the basics of the game in international clubs.

"Coaching tends to be centrally structured through national federations, with an emphasis on fundamentals and teamwork," writes Longman. "Exposure to international play is high, beginning at the youth level. And global players often turn professional at an age when American players are just qualifying for their driver's license. Splitter, San Antonio's Brazilian center, signed his first pro contract at 15."

This global talent pool is clearly an advantage for the Spurs. Identifying talent in global markets gives the team high-caliber players that would otherwise be missed by domestic scouts. Popovich was able to exploit the lack of international scouting to his advantage because other teams had certain biases when it came to foreign players.

Back in the 1990s, and even to certain extent in today's NBA, there is a common perception of foreign basketball players. Seth Wickersham of ESPN highlights some of the claims made against foreign players. “They wouldn’t play defense, they wouldn’t socialize, they wouldn’t learn English, they weren’t strong dribblers, they couldn’t handle a reduced role, they were soft,” he writes.

Popovich also mentioned some of the common misconceptions against foreign players. The New York Times wrote that many executives in the NBA thought that they were “uncoachable because they did not fit in socially, grew homesick, did not speak English fluently and did not play defense. There also seemed to be a reluctance to travel widely to scout global players.”

“All those things together formed a prejudice,” Popovich stated. These biases and cultural misunderstanding caused executives around the league to ignore players that could have contributed to the team's success. “I thought that was really ignorant,” Popovich told ESPN about how international players were viewed. “I couldn’t believe that it was a pool that wasn’t being used.”

Reaching out to untapped areas to find talent isn’t limited to players. Gregg Popovich and the Spurs also hires coaches from a wider pool of talent. Popovich’s top assistant in the 2014-2015 season was Ettore Messina, who is widely considered to be one of the best coaches in Europe. Messina won 4 Euroleague championships along with numerous Coach of the Year awards in Italy and across Europe.

Another coaching hire that Popovich made was hiring Becky Hammon to be the first full-time, paid female assistant on a NBA coaching staff. Hammon was a former star in the WNBA and was looking to get into coaching. Hammon interned with the Spurs during the 2013-2014 season, and impressed Popovich with her basketball intelligence.

“Having observed her working with our team this past season, I’m confident her basketball IQ, work ethic and interpersonal skills will be a great benefit to the Spurs,” Popovich said in a released statement on the hire.

The Spurs organization looked past the gender issue and was able to determine that in coaching, the mind is much more important than physical strength, as Hammon stated to ESPN.

"As far as women coaching men, it's really silly," Hammon said. "People ask me all the time, will there ever be a woman player in the NBA? To be honest, no. There are differences. The guys are too big, too strong and that's just the way it is.

"But when it comes to things of the mind, things like coaching, game-planning, coming up with offensive and defensive schemes, there's no reason why a woman couldn't be in the mix and shouldn't be in the mix."

The Spurs were able to avoid any biases, prejudices, or misconceptions about women in leadership positions to hire Becky Hammon. They didn't let the fact that there has never been a female coach in the NBA stop them from hiring someone who they thought was the best person for the job.

But they also didn't hire Hammon simply because she was a woman. Based on the public statements made by the Spurs and people familiar with their thinking, they really do just view her as a coach. They aren't attempting to publicize the fact that she is the first female coach in the NBA. As Nancy Lieberman, a former WNBA star who serves as an executive in the Development League stated, "That's not who they are. They don't do this for the record-breaking barrier."

"I'm sure he didn't hire her because she was a woman," Lieberman continued. "I'm sure he hired her because she was the best person for the job."

This statement proved to be true very quickly, as the Spurs named Hammon the head coach of their summer league team. Hammon coached the team to a championship during the 2015 Summer League.

Gregg Popovich, RC Buford, and the entire Spurs organization constantly look past common perceptions to find the best person for the job. It doesn't matter if they are a player from Brazil, a coach from Italy, or a female in the United States. They will analyze the situation and tap into any resource that will help their organization.

Once Popovich has these players and staff from around the world, he must coach them to play as a cohesive unit. He must get a group of international players from different cultures and lifestyles to work together at a high level. In order to learn how he does that, it's important to first learn a little about his background.

Popovich's Background

As Longman stated, "San Antonio's basketball worldview reflects the curiosity, open-mindedness and acumen of Gregg Popovich." It is fairly safe to say that there is no other coach in the NBA who has had the educational and life experiences of Gregg Popovich.

After growing up in Indiana, Popovich entered the Air Force Academy and graduated with a degree in Soviet Studies in 1970. In a great profile of Popovich in Sports Illustrated, Jack McCallum writes about the intrigue of Popovich, who served as an intelligence office in Eastern Europe.

Was Popovich a spy? "He did have intelligence training, he did apply for a top-secret government job in Moscow (the paperwork was delayed and he didn't get it) and he did briefly serve as an intelligence officer in eastern Turkey, on the borders of Iran and Syria," writes McCallum.

Popovich has stated that although he was stationed at the border, he insists that he wasn't running agents like a Hollywood action hero. As he told Jan Hubbard in *The History of the San Antonio Spurs*, "People had me carrying guns like I was some kind of spy. The more I would deny it, the more they'd roll their eyes and say, 'Yeah, sure. Come on.' I was stationed on the border, but it wasn't like I was James Bond."

After Europe, Popovich was posted to Moffett Federal Airfield in Northern California. While stationed there, Popovich began a lifelong love affair with wine. “Napa Valley was just exploding as a center for wine and food. Myself and a buddy could head up there, hit the wineries, pretty cheap, no crowds. That’s where I started to learn about wine, and from wine you learn about food.”

The first head coaching job that Gregg Popovich had was at Pomona-Pitzer, two colleges in California that share one athletic department. The team played against other small liberal arts schools in California in the NCAA Division III, which means that the players are not offered athletic scholarships. These schools are highly regarded for their academics, and Popovich fully embraced the college environment.

While serving as an Associate Professor at Pomona, Popovich moved his wife and their two children into the college dorms for a year to soak up the atmosphere. He also took an active role in campus wide matters by sitting in on numerous committees.

“I chaired the committee that investigated fraternities,” Popovich told McCallum in Sports Illustrated. “I was scared s__less going in, but the dean wanted someone from athletics who wouldn’t pussyfoot around. We made a lot of changes with the way frats were operating.”

Popovich also played a role in women’s issues on campus. Keep in mind that this was in the 1980s when Popovich was addressing these issues. “I was a member of the women’s commission, too. We looked into issues of gender equality, discrimination against gays, abuses in athletics. Those kinds of things are what I really enjoyed.”

In 1986, Popovich took his sabbatical that is given to professors. Popovich used his sabbatical to intern with Larry Brown, who was then coaching at the University of Kansas. The Kansas Jayhawks are one of college basketball’s powerhouses, with a long history of winning. The Allen Fieldhouse, where the team plays, is considered one the most historic and important arenas in college basketball. The court is named for James Naismith, who invented basketball and established the program at Kansas.

After his sabbatical, Popovich scheduled a game with Kansas the following year so that his players could have the experience of playing in Allen Fieldhouse. His team lost 94-38. That year, the Jayhawks would go on to win the national championship.

One of the key traits of Gregg Popovich that emerged during this time is his curiosity about the world. Steven Koblik, a friend of Popovich and the Former President of Reed College in Portland, told Sports Illustrated that the combination of interests and smarts in Gregg Popovich creates a unique mind.

“It is not sufficient to say merely that Gregg is smart. He is also intellectually curious,” Koblick told the magazine. “Now, you combine that with basketball smarts and street smarts and add someone who’s a very good judge of people, and that makes for a very unusual person.”

Gaining Trust With Players

With his wide range of interests, Popovich is able to be well-informed on many different topics and issues. This curiosity of the world allows him to be able to create connections with his players, no matter their background. As the coach of the team, Popovich understands that it's his responsibility to connect with his players, to bring them into the Spurs culture, and to make sure that they have a strong relationship with him and the other players.

One way that he does that is by talking to them about things outside of basketball. By talking to them about their interests and their life outside of the court, he shows the players that he truly does care about them. This interest in their lives creates the foundation for their solid relationship.

Here are just a few reported incidents of how Popovich shows he cares about his players.

- He discusses Argentine politics and political conspiracies with Manu Ginobili.
- He handed out DVDs of the 2012 presidential debate to all of his players.
- Popovich flew to the island of St. Croix to get to know Tim Duncan before the draft in 1997.
- He was with Tony Parker in London after the September 11 attacks prevented Parker from flying out of the city immediately.
- There was a time when Hedo Turkoglu, native of Turkey, and Rasho Nesterovic, from Slovenia, were on the team. Popovich would talk to both players in broken Serbian.

When discussing how Popovich talked in Serbian to his two players, General Manager RC Buford stated that it was just one example of how Popovich attempts to build relationships with his players.

“That’s something that those guys don’t get a lot of places. It just adds to the relationship. It doesn’t cement it, but it sures puts it in a different perspective. Those guys know he is making an attempt to be one of them,” Buford told the NY Times.

The foundation that he creates with his players by making the effort to connect with them allows Popovich to be very clear and direct with his players. Since everyone clearly knows that Popovich is coming from a good place, they are open to his teaching. They become “coachable” because they have already seen that Popovich really does have their best interests at heart. As former player Robert Horry said, “Pop just wants the best out of you. He’s going to be on you hard, I mean really hard, so if you have the mental toughness to take that, you’re going to develop as a player.”

The directions and coaching that Popovich gives to his players can seem harsh to outsiders, but all of the players fully embrace it. For example, during the 2014 championship season, Popovich was asked about Patty Mills, who was in the midst of a breakout season that year. When asked what happened to lead Mills to play at a much higher level, Popovich had this to say, as recorded by mysanantonio.com:

"He was a little fat ass. He had too much junk in the trunk. His decision making wasn't great, and he wasn't in great shape. He changed his entire body. He came back svelte and cut and understood you have to make better decision, point-guard type decisions. He did all those things better and he earned it. He's been real important to us, obviously."

Later, Patty Mills was asked by Jim Rome what he thought about Popovich calling him "a little fat ass" in public, and Mills had no problem with it.

"That's nothing compared to what I've heard. I took that as a compliment," Mills laughed as he told Jim Rome on his show. "No, it was all good mate. Obviously, I knew what I had to do to make a contribution to this team and I thought that last summer was a big summer for me to correct those things and basically just put me in the best possible position to be on the team."

Regardless of their status, Popovich will let them know if they messed up. "He was always screaming at me, like he was hard to take sometimes, getting all red and getting crazy," says All-Star Point Guard Tony Parker. "Now, we've got a great relationship and we understand each other. He's pretty flexible and you have to give him credit for that because he adapts to my style of playing and Manu's style."

Manu Ginobili has also been on the receiving end of Popovich's wrath. "You get worried because there's a vein here that just gets so big, you think it's going to explode," he says. But he also understands that it isn't personal, and that it really is for the betterment of the team.

“He’s a smart coach. He knows how to get the best from his team. He’s got that temperament that he gets very upset, and he’s not afraid to tell anything to anybody. He doesn’t care if it’s Tim Duncan or the player that is on the I.R. So everybody feels the same situation. I think it’s really good for the spirit of the team,” Ginobili says.

Assistant coach Ettore Messina wrote that the demanding nature of Popovich’s personality is based upon the care that he has for everyone in the organization.

“Coach Popovich has this rare ability to combine his demanding nature with the most sincere care for everybody in the organization,” writes Messina. “Players, management, coaches, doctors, physiotherapists - he cares about all of them. And that makes everyone proud to be a part of the organization.”

“This is family first, basketball club second.”

Review Questions:

1. How is the performance model for your team or personal goals? The business performance model consists of Strategy, Structure, People and Process.

- What is your strategy? What is the blueprint that you will follow to achieve your goals? A strategy is not a mission statement, or a statement where you say you will "Work Hard". You need to have a specific plan on how you will achieve your goals.
- Do you have a structure to implement your strategy? Are you organized in a way that will allow you to commit to your strategy?
- Do you have the right people helping you reach your goal? Are they capable of doing what you need them to accomplish? Do you have the right tools and resources you need to implement your strategy?
- Do you have the right process for your strategy? Do you have the right reward systems in place? Is everyone on the same page? How's your team culture?

2. Where are you finding your players, workers, or talent? How are you promoting within your staff or team? Could it be possible that you may be overlooking some people due to unknown biases? Whether it be due to age, gender, or background, are you sure you are not allowing previous ideas to prevent you from finding the best possible candidate? It doesn't even have to be something as obvious as race or gender. Your bias could be something more subtle. Remember, the NBA didn't want to draft international players because they thought they were "soft". Maybe you think that managers must come out of the sales department, and that people in accounting aren't management material. Be sure to keep your eyes open for talent in all places.

3. How is your relationship with other members of your team? Do you have a good relationship? Popovich wouldn't be considered a "friend" by his players, but they do know that he cares about them as people. He does this by talking to them about things other than basketball. Do you reach out to members of your staff and talk to them about other interests? Do you know what some of your teammates hobbies are? By talking to them about other topics, it shows them that you care about them as a person. This connection is the foundation of trust and lies at the heart of team building.

Part 2: Performance

"Pound the Rock"

Gregg Popovich isn't big on motivational slogans. He calls them "trite silly crap". However, there is one quote that he does have hanging in the Spurs locker room. With the global nature of the Spurs, the New York Times reported that the quote is also translated to French, Spanish and Portuguese.

Here is the quote by Jacob Riis that plays an important part of Popovich's thinking.

"When nothing seems to help, I go back and look at a stonecutter hammering away at his rock perhaps a hundred times without as much as a crack showing in it. Yet at the hundred and first blow it will split in two, and I know it was not that blow that did it - but all that had gone before."

This quote has been so instrumental to Gregg Popovich that he has named his small wine label Rock and Hammer. The Spurs community has also embraced the quote, with the Spurs blog on SB Nation naming itself *Pounding the Rock*.

The quote itself shows the unique mindset of Popovich, and his wide range of interests. Jacob Riis was a immigrant from Denmark who arrived in New York City as a 21 year old in 1870 with 40 dollars in his pocket. He became a police photographer and became friends with the NYC Police Commissioner and Future President Theodore Roosevelt. After seeing the abject poverty in the neighborhoods, Riis became a social reformer who published a photography book called "How the other half lives."

The Smithsonian writes that the book was full of unapologetically harsh accounts of life in the worst slums of New York, fascinating and terrible statistics on tenement living, and reproductions of his revelatory photographs." The book was so influential that "it inspired Roosevelt to close the worst of the lodging houses and spurred city officials to reform and enforce the city's housing policies."

J.R. Wilco of Pounding the Rock asked Popovich about the quote, and here is his response in full.

Transcribed by Andrew A. McNeill of 48 Minutes of Hell:

"It was back in the 90s and I was reading something about immigration in New York way back when, that kind of thing, and he was a reformer. He fought for better housing and better conditions, working conditions, that type of thing, for immigrants of all countries.

"He was relentless at it and that quote we use is obviously his quote, and I thought it embodied anyone's effort in any endeavor, really. It doesn't have to be basketball. It can be a musical instrument, or it can be learning mathematics or going to law school or figuring out how to turn the water off in your house because you're an idiot. If you can't figure that out you just keep looking, keep trying, keep going.

"The way he said it was very eloquent, and I thought that it fit. You get tired of all that other junk, 'Winners never do this' or 'Losers always quit'. 'There's no I in team' -- all that typical, trite silly crap you see in locker rooms at all levels. It's always turned me off, so I thought that this was maybe a little bit more, I don't know, intelligent. A different way to get the guys and make them think about it."

The emphasis on hard work and doing what is necessary lies at the heart of Gregg Popovich's coaching. As the quote by Riis makes clear, you can't break the rock unless you take all of the steps that are needed. It simply is not possible to skip steps when trying to break a rock, an obstacle, or achieve a championship. You can't go from 27th blow to the 101st blow that breaks the rock. It doesn't work that way.

Assistant coach Ettore Messina lays out the philosophy of Gregg Popovich by saying that "one of the biggest things in coach Popovich's philosophy is the 'we can't skip any steps' principle. It means there's time and place for every process."

In order to not skip any steps, it means that the Spurs must start from the very beginning. As anyone who attempts to master any skill, the fundamentals must be strong before you can advance. And that is exactly what the Spurs do every season.

"You always start from the basics here and then go on to the most intricate things," writes Messina about his time in San Antonio. "At the beginning of the training camp we went over the fundamentals of offense and defense. Passing, catching, pivoting, sliding, moving without the ball - it was as if we were a junior team," he writes.

According to Popovich's thinking, only by having a strong foundation can you be in a position to win. "That's one of the major messages coach Popovich sends out to his players: techniques are much more important than tactics. You have to master the fundamentals and then you need the desire to compete every day, meaning that every day you have to come in ready to play," says Messina.

Once that foundation is built upon, it becomes possible to quickly adapt and change. That's the key objective that all young players in any sport or in any field must realize. Only by having a strong foundation can you then adapt to exploit any weaknesses or opportunities that arise. If the Spurs were unable to be so fundamentally sound, then they wouldn't be able to change their offensive style from their first championship in 1999 to their latest trophy in 2014.

Adaptability

One of the keys to the Spurs long-lasting success has been their ability to adapt to the environment. Whether the changes were brought upon by new basketball strategies or through rule changes, Popovich and the Spurs has been able to adjust.

Popovich won his first NBA championship in 1999. He won his fifth NBA title in sixteen years later in 2014. He took over the coaching job for the Spurs for the 1996-1997 season, when they missed the playoffs. Since then, the Spurs has been in the playoffs every year since the 1997-1998 season, or 18 straight years.

During those years, the NBA has changed drastically. When he won his first title in 1998, the Spurs had two 7 footers on their rosters. David Robinson and Tim Duncan served as the anchor of the team. The Spurs were able to play solid defense and utilized the size of the two big men. The game back then was more physical, with a heavy emphasis on defense and post-up plays by the two big men.

By the time the Spurs won the title in 2014, the NBA has changed drastically. Sports analytics and advanced statistics have changed not just the way the game is played, but the type of players that are valuable. From shooting more threes to spacing on offense, the style of play in NBA games has evolved from the bruising battles of the 1980s and 1990s.

"You got to keep up with it, because teams change, players' careers change and the makeup of the team changes," Popovich told the Washington Post. "Standing pat never works."

In addition, the NBA made a big rule change for the 2004-2005 season when they outlawed hand-checking. The defender no longer could place their hands on the offensive player while defending him. This rule change allowed the offensive player to be able to drive to the basket, creating more scoring opportunities.

Like any successful CEO who deals with new regulations, Gregg Popovich was able to adapt to these new rules faster than his competitors.

Nate Scott of USA Today highlights the championships that the Spurs won, and how Popovich has always been able to adapt as necessary. Scott writes that the first championship was built "around the two 7-footers and a bevy of defenders and shooters. When Robinson's body started breaking down, Popovich redesigned the team, giving more responsibility to a young Manu Ginobili to create around the perimeter. The Spurs won the 2002/2003 NBA title."

After those two titles, the NBA changed its hand checking rules, so "Popovich immediately incorporated a 22-year old Tony Parker into the offense, using the speedy point guard to penetrate into the lane and create scoring opportunities for Duncan and Ginobili, along with other veteran defenders and shooters on the team."

The Spurs won the championships in 2005 and 2007. Despite making the playoffs each year, the Spurs wouldn't win their 5th title until 2014. For that title, "Popovich was able to rebuild his team, this time with a heavy emphasis on wing players who could defend and hit 3-pointers," writes Scott.

"Everyone knows now that was the direction the NBA was heading in. Popovich just saw it before anyone else."

This ability to notice the changes and adapt his system to exploit those changes is one of the key traits that Popovich has. Scott states that Popovich "can take new information (the change in the hand-checking rules, realizing the efficiency of corner 3s) and instantly incorporate it into his teams style."

"Popovich has managed to do both. He has consistently changed the Spurs' system of play to exploit new rules or trends in the NBA, then drilled the talent he has to fit that system," writes Scott in the USA Today. "He is both a visionary and a pragmatist, and those are really hard to be at the same time."

Empower Staff and Players to Communicate

Another key reason for the ability of the Spurs to change their game strategies is due to Popovich's desire for debate. Although he seems like the gruff, military man who doesn't like people to question his authority, he is actually very open-minded. Popovich encourages his players and his staff to constantly offer their suggestions and ideas to make the team better.

"The Spurs do things together," says assistant coach Messina. "There's a lot of respect for everybody, and everybody is expected to give his or her opinion and help the group. It's a unique philosophy of working together and facing adversity together as well."

Messina goes on to describe the way Popovich encourages dialogue, discussion, and insight when crafting game plans. "What's interesting is that he always pushes his coaching staff to argue with him. Sometimes he reminds me one of those Greek philosophers, the sophists, who tried to find the truth through arguments. He really encourages discussion and variety of opinions, seeing them as a means to improve as a unit."

In addition to allowing his coaches to express their opinions, Popovich has setup his offensive system to give the players an incredible amount of responsibilities. He wants his players to be smart enough to be able to figure things out on the court. He wants them to be in charge of their own actions and to be able to attack a weakness when they see it. As he told the San Antonio Express-News, "I don't have 14 timeouts."

Popovich wants his players to communicate not just with him but with each other. "You guys got to get together and talk. You guys might see a mismatch that I don't see. You guys need to communicate constantly - talk, talk, talk to each other about what's going on on the court," he says.

He also mentions to the Express-News that there are times during a timeout where he flat-out tells them that there is nothing he can do. If they are messing up, then it's on them to figure out how to fix it.

“Sometimes in timeouts I’ll say ‘I’ve got nothing for you. What do you want me to do? We just turned it over six times. Everybody’s holding the ball. What else do you want me to do here? Figure it out.’ And I’ll get up and walk away. Because it’s true. There’s nothing else I can do for them. I can give them some bulls---, and act like I’m a coach or something, but it’s on them.”

“If they’re holding the ball, they’re holding the ball. I certainly didn’t tell them to hold the ball. Just like, if they make five in a row, I didn’t do that. If they get a great rebound, I didn’t do that. It’s a player's’ game and they’ve got to perform. The better you can get that across, the more they take over and the more smoothly it runs.”

For a coach to say that there are times where he can’t do anything for the team takes a lot of confidence . A rookie head coach in the NBA will probably never tell the team during a timeout to “figure it out” and walk away.

But Popovich is able to do this because he has built up a system that allows for this type of thinking by the players. He isn’t being lazy, or attempting to pass on his responsibilities as a head coach. Rather, he understands that in the fast moving NBA, communication and self-empowerment by the players is very important to winning.

“I think that communication thing really helps them,” he says. “It engenders a feeling that they can actually be in charge. I think competitive character people don’t want to be manipulated constantly to do what one individual wants them to do. It’s a great feeling when players get together and do things as a group. Whatever can be done to empower those people,” says Popovich.

He is also clear with the Express-News that coaching is still necessary. He doesn’t just throw the ball at them and tell them to think up a play. “You interject here or there. You call a play during the game at some point or make a substitution, that kind of things that helps the team win. But they basically have to take charge or you never get to the top of the mountain.”

Eric Freeman of Yahoo Sports comments about Popovich's thinking by saying that it has "led him to treat his players like grown men with their own emotional and professional needs, not models to be molded to his particular needs."

"By realizing that he only has so much control over what happens on the court, Popovich has reached the reasonable conclusion that he must make his players especially confident that they can accomplish their goals without much outside help," writes Freeman. "He's giving them ownership of the offense effectively by telling them that they are the ones responsible for winning and losing. He's empowering his players, or at least allowing them in a position to grab the power if they want it."

Resiliency

The ability to bounce back from disappointment is a skill that everyone needs to develop. No matter how hard we try, we will face losses, failures, and utter disappointments in life. Popovich and the Spurs have dealt with heartbreaking losses, but they have also learned how to be resilient.

Popovich is one of the most successful coaches in the NBA with 5 championships. However, he has been coaching the Spurs for 19 seasons. That means that for 14 seasons, he has ended the year losing a playoff round. Anyone in a competitive industry must accept the fact that winning is simply not possible each year.

"You think you're on the Earth and everything you want to happen to you is going to happen to you positively? The measure of who we are is how we react to something that doesn't go our way," he told JA Adande of ESPN.

Perhaps the most difficult loss came in 2013, when the Spurs lost to the Miami Heat in the NBA Finals. While leading the series with a 3 games to 2 lead, the Spurs were close to winning the championship in Game Six. With just 28 seconds remaining, the Spurs were leading by 5 points. NBA officials brought out the yellow tape and was preparing for the championship trophy presentation on the sidelines.

However, the Spurs failed to get a defensive rebound, allowing Miami to shoot a three-pointer to tie the game and forcing overtime. The Heat were able to win the game in overtime, setting the stage for a winner take all Game 7. In the decisive game, with 50 seconds left in the fourth quarter, Tim Duncan had a chance to tie the game, yet missed the shot and the put back. Lebron James was able to score on the other end, and the Miami Heat sealed the victory and the championship.

Losing the Finals was clearly devastating for the Spurs. A popular discussion on sports media in the days that followed focused on how heart-wrenching the loss must be for Gregg Popovich and the Spurs. Popovich was criticized for keeping Tim Duncan on the bench in the final seconds of Game 6, when the Spurs were unable to grab a rebound that lead to the 3 pointer.

The next year however, the Spurs were able to bounce back from being so close and reach the NBA finals again. Every player spent the entire season dedicated to the goal of reaching the finals. At the end of the 2014 season, Spurs had the best record season record in the NBA.

In the NBA finals, they met up again with the Miami Heat. After splitting the first two games of the series, the Spurs then went on a historic run, absolutely demolishing the Heat to win the series in 5 games.

It was clearly a nice redemption story about the Spurs. However, when Adande talked about the resiliency of the Spurs, Popovich offered a different take.

To Popovich, the narrative that the Spurs were able to bounce back and get revenge by winning the 2014 champions was completely missing the point.

“In today’s world, if you don’t win the whole thing, whether it’s football or basketball, or this and that, people have a tendency to paint you as a loser or act like you just robbed the cookie jar,” he told ESPN. “Well that’s baloney.”

To Popovich, the true story about the Spurs wasn’t the 2014 championship, but Game 7 of the 2013 NBA Finals. After failing to close out the Heat in Game 6, the Spurs were able to come back 2 days later and still compete. That was the real story. That was the true display of character, will, and a champion mindset.

“I’m just as proud of them in the loss as I was this year in the win,” Popovich says about his team. “I thought when they came back in Game 7 (in 2013), that was an unbelievable effort after that devastating loss in Game 6.”

Adande sums up how everyone simply glossed over the resiliency shown in Game 7. “We missed the target. We’re so focused on the Hollywood ending, with the confetti raining down on the Spurs in San Antonio a year later, that we’ve forgotten about the fortitude they showed in losing Game 7 in Miami,” he writes. “The Spurs seemed too emotionally depleted right after Game 6 to put up another fight. And yet they shook it all off to play an ultra-competitive Game 7, a contest that never swayed beyond a two-possession game until Miami’s Dwyane Wade made a free throw with 16.3 seconds left to provide the final 95-88 score.”

“If we only praise the Spurs for winning in 2014 and not for the way they played in defeat in 2013, then we’re right back where we started, making the same mistake of obsession over winning while writing off the losers and failing to acknowledge their accomplishments. Game 7 was their real triumph. That’s when they showed their character in adversity. It’s what convinced Popovich that they could make a run at it next season.”

But how did they make that run? How did Popovich teach a group of individuals to bounce back? To stay motivated towards a goal for an entire year after facing a huge disappointment can be very difficult. The constant thoughts of "what could have been" and of regret has led to many individuals and teams imploding the following year. So how did the Spurs manage to stay focused and bounce back from heartbreak?

There were two key lessons that Popovich told his players.

1. You are in control of the situation.

Popovich stressed to the players that they are in charge of their own self-determination. They are the ones who control their lives, their efforts, and their mindset. With that belief firmly ingrained into his players mind, they were able to work to improve their play and put themselves back into a competitive mindset.

Popovich explained how he got his players to take control of their emotions, thoughts and actions. "What we didn't want to do is have them have the notion that the basketball gods got us. 'Ah jeez, that one bounce here or we missed a free throw or we didn't get that offensive rebound. It's just the way it was supposed to be.' Well, no, it's got nothing to do with the basketball gods. You're in charge of yourself. There are always things you can do better," he says.

The way that Popovich got his players to get over the loss was to focus on what they could control. Don't focus on how close you were to the championship, but focus on the actions you took. Focusing on the lost opportunity does nothing for the player. It just makes them frustrated, sad, and living in the past. Rather, Popovich had his players focus on things that they can improve on and things that were still in their control.

"It's a game of mistakes," Popovich said. "That's why people score, because you make mistakes. So let's figure out what we could have done, and that makes us a better team."

"We went through every single play of Game 6 and Game 7. We made them sit through it. We didn't yell and scream at 'em or berate 'em or anything. We were very businesslike. 'Here's where we didn't give help. Here's where we didn't rebound or put five men on the board.' So we understand it's on us. And now you can move forward."

By focusing on things that they could improve upon, the Spurs took control of their own destiny. Rather than moping about how close they were, Popovich gave them things to do. The players had things to focus on. They could be productive by working on specific things. Their minds had a new task to concentrate on, rather than thinking about the past.

"It's on us to see what we can do to get back into that same position," Popovich said. "Can we or can't we? We may, or we may not. I have no clue. But we can put out the effort both mentally and physically to have the best shot to get there. And that's what guided us the whole year, that philosophy. We didn't worry about how many wins. We just worried about being healthy and continuing to improve on all the things that we saw in Game 6 and 7. And to their credit, they showed the fortitude to do that."

2. Gratitude of being able to compete.

The second message that Popovich gave his players was to remind them of the incredible opportunity they had to be able to compete for a championship, let alone play basketball for a living. He reminded them that even though they may have fell a little short of winning the championship, they were still very fortunate to even have the opportunity to play at the biggest stage.

"We spend a decent amount of time talking about what else you could be doing in your life, how fortunate we are basically just by the accident of birth," he said. "Think about it. It all starts with the accident of birth. Because you were born to these parents or this area geographically, or this situation, you deserve more than somebody else? Put that notion away. That's the most false notion one can imagine."

“But I think a lot of people forget that. They think that they’re entitled to what they have. They don’t understand the opportunity that they have compared to somebody else. And they don’t understand the other person’s lack of opportunity, why he or she is in a certain situation they’re in. So we talk about all those things all the time.”

Understanding how fortunate a person is, and expressing gratitude in being able to compete, should give a person all the motivation they need, according to Popovich. “You have no excuse not to work your best. You have no reason not to be thankful every day that you have the opportunity to come back from a defeat, because some people never even have the opportunity.”

Review Questions:

1. Are you pounding the rock? Are you putting in the work and not skipping any steps? It's tempting to find shortcuts or "hacks" that promise to make us more productive in less time. All too often, we tell ourselves that we are working smarter, but really we are just being lazy. The Spurs go over the fundamentals at the start of every training camp and puts in the time and effort to be successful. Although the 101 blow to the rock may break it, you need those first 100 blows to get it in position to break.

2. How are you adapting to changes in your field? Whether it be new technology, regulations, or even ideas, every industry is seeing changes occur at a rapid pace. Methods that were successful 5 years ago may no longer be working as your competitors would have adjusted. Have you made any changes to your strategy or work habits in recent years? How often do you review your skill set to see if you need to learn new things? When was the last time you learned a new skill or technique?

3. Are you able to bounce back from defeat? Do you think that you must win every time, and get upset, angry or emotional when things don't go your way? Do you always focus on the goals that you weren't able to get? Remember, the keys to being resilient is to focus on the steps that you control.

Conclusion

During the 2005 NBA Finals, the New York Times had a great story that captures the essence of Gregg Popovich and the San Antonio Spurs.

The Spurs were about to start the championship series against the defending champs Detroit Pistons. As was his style, Popovich was attempting to keep the mood light for his team. One of his methods is to talk about current events that are taking place outside of basketball.

So Popovich asked his team of professional basketball players from around the world if they watched the national spelling bee that took place earlier. "I wanted to know if anybody knew the word that won," Popovich told Liz Robbins of the Times. "It was appoggiatura."

While attempting to talk about the contest, Popovich had to explain the contest three times to his team. The reason for the confusion was due to the international makeup of his team.

"Manu was like, 'Spelling bee? Where are the bees'", Popovich said.

Rather than get frustrated at the misunderstanding, Popovich relishes it. Having talented players who are smart, coachable, and committed to winning are worth any communication challenges that he may face. "Most people just didn't believe it, they didn't want foreign kids, thinking they didn't speak English and it's going to be a pain," Popovich said.

This little interaction between one of his top players and Gregg Popovich is a perfect example of how the team culture is. Before Game 1 of the NBA Finals, Popovich is talking about the spelling bee to his players. One of his star players is showing the same level of curiosity and engagement by continually asking his coach to explain the concept of a "spelling bee". The reason that the player doesn't understand what the "bee" represents is because the player is from Argentina and the Spurs finds talent anywhere in the world.

Clearly, this culture that Popovich created in San Antonio is effectively, because they went on to win the championship that year.

Gregg Popovich has won 5 championship titles as of 2015 by caring about his players. He solidifies his relationships by being interested in their lives, their values, and their beliefs. As he told Jack McCallum of Sports Illustrated, that is one of the key reasons for the Spurs continued success.

"Relationships with people are what it's all about. You have to make players realize you care about them. And they have to care about each other and be interested in each other. Then they start to feel a responsibility toward each other. Then they want to for each other," Popovich said.

"And I have always though it helps if you can make it fun, and one of the ways you do that is let them think you're a little crazy, that you're interested in things outside of basketball. 'Are there weapons of mass destruction? Or aren't there? What, don't you read the papers?'"

"You have to give the message that the world is wider than a basketball court."

Keys Takeaways

1. Have a strategy, a structure to implement that strategy, the people who can carry out that strategy, and the process to accomplish it.

2. Stability in management and within the organization can be beneficial. If you have the right people in place, a culture of excellence can grow.

3. In order to avoid stagnation, debate and new ideas must always be allowed. This is especially the case when a core group of people have been with the team for a long period of time.

4. There is talent in overlooked places. Be sure to notice any biases that you may have when selecting people.

5. Pay attention to the rules and regulations of your field. If you can adjust to them quicker than others, you'll be able to gain an advantage.

6. Being aware of issues and topics outside of your field is not a waste of time. It allows you to be curious about other people's lives, which serves as the foundation of a trusting relationship.

7. Technique is more important that tactics. Having strong fundamentals allows your team to be able to adjust and adapt quickly.

8. There is no skipping steps. You must put in the work.

9. Focus on what you can control and improve upon. Don't let missed chances, closed defeats, or heartbreaking losses linger in your mind. Focus on the specific things you can do to improve.

10. Be grateful for the opportunities you have to compete.

About Leadership Case Studies

Leadership Case Studies provides brief reports and analysis on successful individuals. We focus on the habits, strategies, and mindsets of high-performing people in the sports, business, and entertainment industries.

Started in July 2015, Leadership Case Studies released its first case study on University of Alabama Football Coach Nick Saban, winner of 4 national championships.

Website:
http://www.leadershipcasestudies.com

Additional Leadership Case Studies

The Team Building Strategy of Steve Kerr

The Strategy Concepts of Bill Belichick

The Turnaround Strategies of Jim Harbaugh

The Management Ideas of Nick Saban

The Motivational Techniques of Urban Meyer

The Work Ethic of Tom Brady, Peyton Manning, and Aaron Rodgers